If you were a

Prefix

by Marcie Aboff
illustrated by Sara Gray

PICTURE WINDOW BOOKS
Minneapolis, Minnesota

prefix a letter or group of letters placed before a word to change its meaning

Editor: Christianne Jones
Designer: Hilary Wacholz
Page Production: Melissa Kes
Art Director: Nathan Gassman
The illustrations in this book were created
with acrylics.

Picture Window Books
1710 Roe Crest Drive
North Mankato, MN 56003
www.capstonepub.com

Library of Congress Cataloging-
in-Publication Data
Aboff, Marcie.
If you were a prefix / by Marcie
Aboff ; illustrated by Sara Gray.
p. cm. — (Word fun)
Includes index.
ISBN-13: 978-1-4048-4773-6
(library binding)
ISBN-13: 978-1-4048-4777-4
(paperback)
ISBN-13: 978-1-4795-8363-8
(saddlestitch)
1. English language—Suffixes and
prefixes—
Juvenile literature. I. Gray, Sara, ill. II.
Title.
PE1175.A23 2008
428.1—dc22   D08006347

Looking for prefixes?

Watch for the underlined letters throughout the book.

Special thanks to our advisers for their expertise:

Rosemary G. Palmer, Ph.D., Department of Literacy
College of Education, Boise State University

Terry Flaherty, Ph.D., Professor of English
Minnesota State University, Mankato

Printed in the United States   5605

If you were a prefix ...

3

... you would come first!

4

Prefixes can make a regular school a <u>pre</u>school, change angles, to <u>tri</u>angles, and make lucky <u>un</u>lucky.

If you were a prefix, you would be a letter or group of letters placed before a word to change its meaning.

The colorful caterpillar <u>trans</u>formed into a <u>multi</u>colored butterfly.

If you were the prefix "re," you could do things over again.

During the _rematch_, the giraffe _re_bounded the ball and dribbled down the path.

8

The monkey had to <u>re</u>play the phone message about <u>re</u>placing the missing bananas.

If you were the prefix "co," you could help do an important job.

The <u>co</u>pilot helped the pilot fly the airplane.

The <u>co</u>-captain helped the captain steer the ship.

If you were the prefix "tele," you could talk to, see, and watch things far away.

The owl called the eagle on the <u>tele</u>phone.

The robin looked for the eagle with a <u>tele</u>scope.

The birds watched their favorite show on <u>television</u>!

13

If you were a prefix, you could give a word added meaning.

The jaguar looked like a star driving his ordinary car.

The jaguar looked like a superstar driving his extraordinary car.

If you were a prefix, you could change the same word in different ways.

You could make a cycle a <u>uni</u>cycle, a <u>bi</u>cycle, or a <u>tri</u>cycle.

If you were a prefix, you could change a word to mean its opposite.

The happy rabbit jumped out of the hole, and his friends appeared.

The <u>un</u>happy rabbit climbed into the hole, and his friends <u>disappeared</u>.

If you were a prefix, you could be yourself. The prefix *pre* means "before." The word *fix* means "to place." *Prefix* means "to place before."

You would always come first ...

Prefix

... if you were a prefix.

FINISH

FUN WITH PREFIXES

Cut out 14 pieces of paper. On each piece of paper, write one of the prefixes or root words from below. Mix them up and see if you can put the words back together. Then make your own list and have a friend match the words. You can even time each other and see who can match the words faster.

mis place
un finished
non sense
mid way
pre view
tele cast
over work

Glossary

extraordinary—more than ordinary

multicolored—having many colors

prefix—a letter or group of letters placed before
    a word to change its meaning

rebounded—to gain possession of the basketball
    after a shot

root—the basic meaning of the word

transformed—changed form

To Learn More

More Books to Read

Draze, Dianne. *Red Hot Root Words.* Austin, Tex.: Dandy Lion
    Publications, 2003.

Heinrichs, Ann. *Prefixes and Suffixes.* Chanhassen, Minn.:
    Child's World, 2006.

Langton, Charan. *Big Words for Little Kids.* San Ramon, Calif.:
    Mountcastle Company, 2007.

On the Web

FactHound offers a safe, fun way to find Web sites
related to topics in this book. All of the sites on
FactHound have been researched by our staff.

1. Visit *www.facthound.com*
2. Type in this special code:
   1404847731
3. Click on the FETCH IT button.

Your trusty FactHound will fetch the best sites for you!

Index

Look for all of the books in the Word Fun series:

If You Were a Compound Word

If You Were a Conjunction

If You Were a Contraction

If You Were a Homonym or a Homophone

If You Were a Noun

If You Were a Palindrome

If You Were a Prefix

If You Were a Preposition

If You Were a Pronoun

If You Were a Suffix

If You Were a Synonym

If You Were a Verb

If You Were Alliteration

If You Were an Adjective

If You Were an Adverb

If You Were an Antonym

If You Were an Interjection

If You Were Onomatopoeia